At Sylvan, we believe reading is one of life's most important and enriching abilities, and we're glad you've chosen our resources to help your child build this critically important skill. We know that the time you spend with your children reinforcing the lessons learned in school will contribute to their love of reading. This love of reading will translate into academic achievement. Successful readers are ready for the world around them, ready to do research, ready to experience the world of literature, and prepared to make the connections necessary to achieve in school and in life.

At Sylvan we use a research-based, step-by-step process in teaching reading that includes thought-provoking reading selections and activities. As students increase their success as readers they become more confident. With increasing confidence, students build even more success. Our Sylvan activity books are designed to help you to help your child build the skills and confidence that will contribute to your child's success in school.

Included with your purchase of this activity book is a coupon for a discount at a participating Sylvan center. We hope you will use this coupon to further your child's academic journey. To learn more about Sylvan and our innovative in-center programs, call 1-800-EDUCATE or visit www.SylvanLearning.com.

We look forward to partnering with you to support the development of a confident, well-prepared, independent learner.

The Sylvan Team

Published in the United States by Random House, Inc., New York, and in Canada by Random House of Canada Limited, Toronto.

www.tutoring.sylvanlearning.com

Producer & Editorial Direction: The Linguistic Edge
Writer: Christina Roll
Cover and Interior Illustrations: Duendes del Sur
Layout and Art Direction: SunDried Penguin

First Edition

ISBN: 978-0-307-47949-5
ISSN: 2161-9824

This book is available at special discounts for bulk purchases for sales promotions or premiums. For more information, write to Special Markets/ Premium Sales, 1745 Broadway, MD 6-2, New York, New York 10019 or e-mail specialmarkets@randomhouse.com.

PRINTED IN THE UNITED STATES OF AMERICA

10 9 8 7 6 5 4 3 2 1

Sylvan
Learning sm

1st Grade
Reading Roundup

Compound Words

It Takes Two

A COMPOUND word is made of two words. The two words are put together to make a new word.

WRITE the compound word made from each pair of pictures.

cupcake

starfish

2

dorbell

3

roncoat

4

One Plus One Makes Two

LOOK at the pictures. READ the words in the word box. WRITE the compound word that matches each pair of pictures.

| football | catfish | doghouse | snowman |

+ = doghouse

+ = snowman

catfish

+ = catfish

football

+ = football

One Plus One Makes...One?

A **contraction** is a shortened form of two words. A symbol called an *apostrophe* takes the place of the missing letter or letters.

Examples: is + not = isn't   he + is = he's

READ the sentences. CIRCLE the contraction in each sentence. WRITE the two words that make up each contraction. LOOK at the word box for help.

it is	I will	we are	were not

1. I'll help make the bed. _____

2. I am happy that we're going to the park. _____

3. Do you think it's going to rain today? _____

4. The birds weren't in the nest. _____

It's a Match

DRAW a line from each contraction to the words it came from.

I'll	were not
won't	you will
I'm	I will
it's	will not
weren't	it is
you'll	cannot
they're	do not
don't	they are
can't	I am

Words That Go Together

Stack Up

LOOK at the words and pictures. WRITE the names of the pictures in the correct columns.

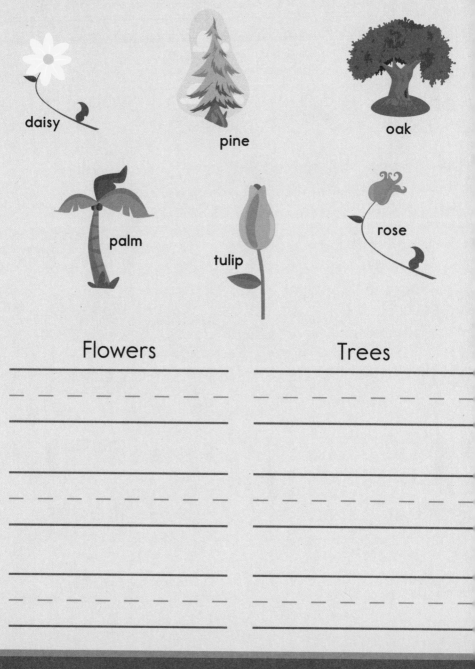

daisy

pine

oak

palm

tulip

rose

Flowers	Trees
_____	_____
_____	_____
_____	_____

Odd Word Out

CIRCLE the picture in each row that does **not** go with the others.

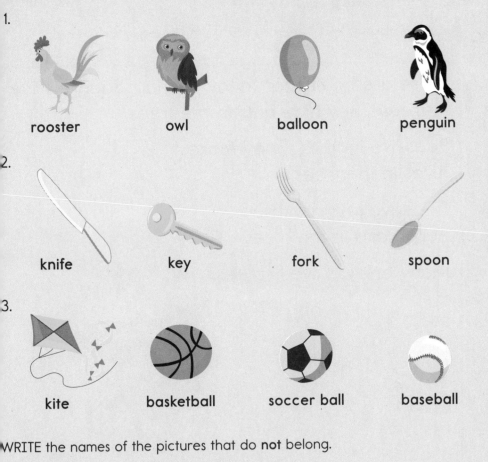

1.

rooster   owl   balloon   penguin

2.

knife   key   fork   spoon

3.

kite   basketball   soccer ball   baseball

WRITE the names of the pictures that do **not** belong.

1

2

3

Name It

The **main idea** is the most important idea in a story. It's the big idea. It tells what the story is about.

READ the stories. CHECK the box next to the best title for each story.

Trees are homes for many animals. Squirrels live in trees. They hide nuts in the trees.

Bees live in trees. They make hives in the trees.

Birds live in trees. They build nests in the trees.

Many animals live in trees.

☐ Bees and Hives

☐ Trees Are Homes

☐ Birds Make Nests

Rosa is a baker. One of the best cakes she ever made was for a man named Mr. Lee. He wanted a special cake for his wife's birthday party. Mrs. Lee loves cats. So Rosa made her a cake with cats on it.

Mrs. Lee thought the cake was the best cake she had ever seen. She did not want to cut it. Mr. Lee said that their guests were waiting to eat cake. Mrs. Lee almost cried when she had to cut the cake. But she loved the way it tasted.

☐ A Special Cake

☐ Cats Are Special

☐ A Birthday Party

What's the Big Idea?

READ the stories. CHECK the sentence that tells the main idea.

Wishes

Have you ever wished for something? My little sister wishes for a new doll and new shoes. My big brother wishes for a computer and a car. I wish that I could fly and travel to the moon. What do you wish for?

☐ People make wishes.

☐ Wishing to fly is better than wishing for a new doll.

☐ You should be happy with what you have.

Buster

Buster likes to do a lot of things. He likes to fetch his rubber ball. He likes to chase butterflies and dig holes. He likes to have his tummy rubbed and his back scratched. But most of all, Buster loves to go for walks in the park.

☐ Buster can fetch a ball.

☐ Buster likes to do many things.

☐ Buster loves to go for walks.

Details, Details

Details tell about the main idea. They can tell who, what, where, when, and how. READ the story. CIRCLE the pictures that show details from the story.

Different but the Same

Lily and Nate are both different and the same. They are different because Lily is tall and Nate is short. Lily plays soccer and Nate plays baseball. Lily has a cat and Nate has a dog. Lily lives in an apartment and Nate lives in a house.

Lily and Nate are the same because Lily likes Nate just the way he is. And Nate likes Lily just the way she is. Lily and Nate say, "That's how friends are."

Who?

What?

Where?

Details, Details

READ the story.

Careful Grace

It was a cold, snowy winter day. Papa and Grace drove a car to the park. They walked to the ice rink inside the park. Papa was going to teach Grace to ice skate.

Papa showed Grace how to put on her skates and how to walk in them. Grace held Papa's hand tightly as the two of them skated around the rink.

At last, Grace let go of Papa's hand. She began to glide on the ice. Papa waved at Grace. She waved back. She hoped that it was not time to stop.

READ each sentence. CIRCLE the picture that matches what happens in the story.

1. How do Papa and Grace get to the park?

2. What kind of day is it?

3. Where did Papa and Grace go?

Yes or No?

READ the story.

Mammals

A mammal is a certain kind of animal. Mammals have hair or fur. Mammals take good care of their babies. Mammals drink their mother's milk.

A tiger is a mammal that lives in the jungles of Asia. Its stripes help it hide in the tall grass.

A pig is a mammal that lives on a farm. It likes to eat corn and roll in the mud.

A bat is a mammal that lives in many places. It can fly.

A whale is a mammal that lives in the ocean. It must come up to breathe air.

Guess what?
You are a
mammal too!

READ each sentence. WRITE **true** if the sentence matches what you read in the story. WRITE **false** if it does not.

1. All mammals have feathers.

   _ _ _ _ _

   _____

2. Pigs like to eat corn.

   _ _ _ _ _

   _____

3. A whale does not need to breathe air.

   _ _ _ _ _

   _____

4. Humans are mammals.

   _ _ _ _ _

   _____

5. Tigers can hide in the tall grass.

   _ _ _ _ _

   _____

Story Order

READ the story.

Hello, Frog!

It's time for newborn frogs! A baby frog is called a tadpole. A tadpole has a large head. Its body is round. It has a long tail. It wiggles its long tail to help it swim. The tadpole grows fast. Its body gets bigger. It grows legs. Then it loses its tail. Now it is a frog.

ow NUMBER the pictures from 1 to 4 to show the order.

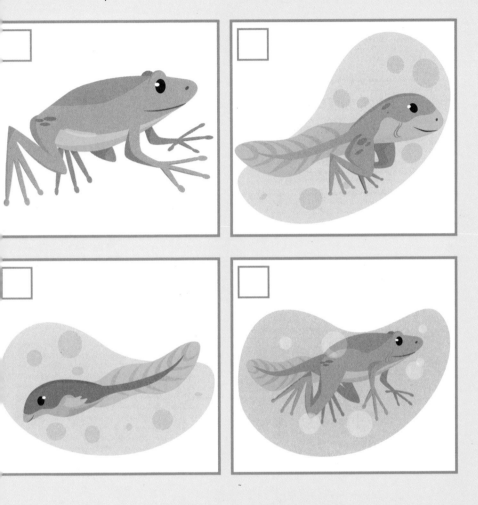

Looking for Clues

Sometimes writers don't tell you everything in a story. You need to look for clues or "read between the lines" to think about what the writer means.

READ each story. LOOK at the picture for clues. FIND the word that best describes the person in the story to complete the sentence.

Jamar is raking leaves.

There are a lot of leaves.

It is hard work.

tired   upset

Jamar feels _____.
1

Marcel got a new bike.

It is big and blue.

He can't wait to ride it.

silly   excited

Marcel feels _____.
2

Annie lost her ring.

She has looked everywhere for it.

Where could it be?

lucky   sad

Annie feels _ _ _ _ _ _ _ .
                    3

Annie found her ring.
It was under her bed.

She puts the ring on her finger.

sleepy   happy

Annie feels _ _ _ _ _ _ _ .
                    4

Looking for Clues

READ each part of the story. THINK about what the writer is saying. Then CIRCLE the correct answer.

Beach Vacation

Jason and Jenna are going to camp at the beach. They help Mom and Dad get ready for the trip. They have to buy food. They have to pack the gear. They have to load the van.

1. Getting ready for a camping trip can be _____.

   a. a lot of work

   b. a waste of time

   c. too easy

The beach is a lot of fun. Jason and Jenna play in the sand. They search for shells. They dig for clams. They swim in the water. They help make the meals. Usually they just have cereal for breakfast and sandwiches for lunch. But for dinner, they fix something special. Jason and Jenna like roasting hot dogs over the fire. Then it is time for bed.

2. What is it like to camp at the beach?

   a. boring

   b. busy

   c. scary

Pick the One

Sometimes you can tell or *predict* what a book is about by looking at the picture on the cover.

LOOK at the picture on each cover. CIRCLE the title that best shows what the story might be about.

 1.

a. *Time to Garden*

b. *Learn to Skate*

c. *Leaves Are Changing*

2.

a. Many Animals Live in Ponds

b. Ducks and Other Birds

c. Frog and Turtle Are Friends

3.

a. Water Play

b. Dog Wash

c. Time to Swim

Fact or Opinion?

A **fact** is something that is true or can be proven. An **opinion** is something that is somebody's own idea.

READ the story. Then READ the sentences on the next page. WRITE **F** if the sentence is a fact. WRITE **O** if the sentence is somebody's opinion.

A Funny Bird

Penguins are interesting birds. Penguins cannot fly. But they can swim fast. They are shaped like a bullet. This helps them swim. They use their wings to move themselves through the water.

Penguins cannot breathe underwater. But they can hold their breath for a long time.

The only time penguins are in the air is when they leap out of the water to get on land. They also jump high into the air to get a gulp of air before diving back down for fish. They look funny when they do this. Penguins are interesting animals.

1. Penguins are interesting birds. _____

2. Penguins cannot fly. _____

3. They use their wings to move
   themselves through the water. _____

4. Penguins cannot breathe underwater.

   _____

5. They look funny when they do this.

   _____

Facts and Opinions

Fact or Opinion?

WRITE **F** if the sentence is a fact. WRITE **O** if the sentence is somebody's opinion.

1. Orange juice tastes good. ____

2. There are seven days in a week. ____

3. Earth has only one moon. ____

4. Blue is the prettiest color. ____

5. Dogs are the best pets ever. ____

6. Roses come in many colors. ____

Answers

Page 2
1. cupcake
2. starfish
3. doorbell
4. raincoat

Page 3
1. doghouse
2. snowman
3. catfish
4. football

Page 4
1. I'll → I will
2. we're → we are
3. it's → it is
4. weren't → were not

Page 5

Page 6
Flowers: daisy, rose, tulip
Trees: pine, oak, palm

Page 7
1. balloon
2. key
3. kite

Page 8
Trees Are Homes

Page 9
A Special Cake

Page 10
People make wishes.

Page 11
Buster likes to do many things.

Page 13

Page 15

Page 17
1. false
2. true
3. false
4. true
5. true

Page 19

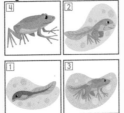

Pages 20–21
1. tired
2. excited
3. sad
4. happy

Pages 22–23
1. a
2. b

Pages 24–25
1. b
2. a
3. b

Page 27
1. O
2. F
3. F
4. F
5. O

Page 28
1. O
2. F
3. F
4. O
5. F

29

770